AN EDITOR'S PET PEEVES
PEEVES
A Pocket Guide for Writers

Debi Staples

Staples, Debi
ISBN: 978-1-7344205-3-1
An Editor's Pet Peeves: A Pocket Guide for
Writers / Debi Staples – 1st ed.

Cover art by Laura Redmond
Edited by Cynthia MacGregor

Printed in the USA

AN EDITOR'S PET PEEVES

TABLE OF CONTENTS

INTRODUCTION
by bf oswald

*Substitute 'damn' every time you're
inclined to write 'very';
your editor will delete it and the writing
will be just as it should be.*
~ Mark Twain

Every print book and every eBook that has been published or will be published (excluding self-publications) is the result of a team effort –a collaboration between an author and an editor as alluded to by Mark Twain.

An editor's primary purpose is to make a good story even better, and let's face the fact – more marketable. An editor is not a destroyer, although a returned manuscript may appear to be decimated by comments and suggested corrections. A good editor does not call your literary baby ugly, but suggests how your creation can be made more attractive.

Every language has rules of grammar, including punctuation, that are understood by the average reader who expects the author to follow them.

2

These rules, I call them mechanics, are the grease that lubricates the wheels of understanding; a rule broken impedes the flow of the sentence and thus interrupts the story.

An editor's job is not proofreading—finding and correcting these mechanical errors; another should do that. An editor's responsibility is to help shape the story by identifying weak areas and offering suggestions about how these can be strengthened. In order to facilitate this process, the submitted draft should be as free of these errors as possible.

An Editor's Pet Peeves should be at the right hand of every author who wants to avoid the mistakes that make an editor groan, and if made in profusion, may cause an editor to reject the work altogether. It is very disappointing to a writer to expend the considerable effort it takes to write a book only to have it disregarded because of too many avoidable errors in punctuation and grammar.

Debi Staples' book is a pocket guide identifying the most common mistakes made by many of the authors she publishes and offering tips on how to identify and correct these mistakes. This treatise is not intended to be a comprehensive compendium of mechanics; the *Chicago Manual of Style* is thus intended, as are several like tomes.

Brief but concise, *Pet Peeves* is well worth the time it takes to read it.

~ bf oswald, Novelist

A book is an arrangement of twenty-six phonetic symbols, ten numerals, and about eight punctuation marks, and people can cast their eyes over these and envision the eruption of Mount Vesuvius or the Battle of Waterloo."

~ Kurt Vonnegut

FOREWORD

"Easy reading is damn hard writing."
~ Nathaniel Hawthorne

So you've written a masterpiece. Congratulations! Now what? "I send it off to be published, of course," you might say. But that is not actually the best answer. A better answer would be "Now I have it edited."

An editor can be a writer's best friend or worst enemy. The right editor can help you turn a good story into a fantastic story. Often, an editor sweats alongside you from the first written page, on to all the rest of the books you write throughout your career. Or an acquisitions editor may simply read the first page of your manuscript, see too many mistakes, and throw all your hard work into the rejection pile without a second thought.

When you submit your work to a magazine, newspaper, or publishing house, in most cases the first person to read your work is an editor... the one person who may or may not pass your work on to the publisher.

In this technological age, where tweeting and texting have become the norm – where shortcuts and abbreviations have become household words – don't fool yourself into believing that it's the storyline itself that will make it or break it for you. In most cases, a well-edited article or manuscript can mean the difference between publication and rejection, even if the storyline itself can still use a little tweaking. You could have written the greatest story or article in the world, but it may never get published if you do not write it up to the standards of an editor.

I am all for writing because you are simply passionate about the craft. But when it comes down to it, if you want your work to be published, it has to be written well.

So I created this book of quick hints and tips to get you started down the road to publication – or, for those of you who have been writing for years, to improve on your current and future works, as I believe it's never too late to learn something new. Of course, there are many books out there on grammar, punctuation, and other technical aspects of writing – and I suggest you take a writing class if at all possible – but this book can show you some of the most common structural problems writers make that are "pet peeves" editors have, which could make the difference between your book being chosen over the next guy's or its being passed over. And for good measure, I've added a few tips for some of the most common grammar and punctuation problems seen in manuscripts today. It's always best to be prepared, especially in today's very competitive publication market.

My wish for you: May your work come back with very little RED (for those of you who remember the days when we used to write on paper and the teacher would mark our mistakes in red ink).

Debi Staples,
Editor & Publisher

STRUCTURE AND FORM

*Writing teaches itself in the act of writing –
but only after you learn the technique
do you find out that writing well is not
about technique at all.*

~ David Gerald

AND THEN….

The word "and" is an important conjunction in writing, but it is often very much overused. And combining it with "then" is redundant. In most instances, the words "and" or "then" are interchangeable, meaning one or the other can be used. But using both is not recommended. Another option is to use neither, replacing them with a simple comma. (Whichever one you use most, try to use that throughout the manuscript instead of making them interchangeable.) The only time I would recommend – or more aptly, expect – the use of "and then" is in dialogue, more specifically when someone is telling a story.

EXAMPLE:
"I turned off my flashlight and then I heard someone scream…"

Also, please do not fall into the trap of using "and then" to extend your sentences.

Sometimes it's much better to start a new sentence then to have "and then" added more than once.

EXAMPLE:
Incorrect: *She came and then she saw and then she conquered.*
Correct: *She came. She saw. She conquered.*

LARGE INDENTATIONS

This is more of a personal preference for me as an editor. When I see a manuscript with paragraph indentations of more than three spaces, it annoys me. It just doesn't look aesthetically pleasing to the eye. I've been told that the standard format for manuals is five indentations, and that's fine – if you're writing a manual. So it's not wrong to use the larger indentation, but make sure to check the submission guidelines of the magazine or publishing house that you're submitting to see if they have a preference before you commit an unwitting mistake.

INDENTING AND DOUBLE SPACING

Very quickly, if you're going to indent your paragraphs, don't double-space between them as well. It's unnecessary and redundant and shows that you are not professional. Whether you double-space between paragraphs or choose to indent each paragraph, do just one or the other and be consistent throughout!

KNOW YOUR CHARACTERS

Once of my biggest pet peeves when I read a manuscript is not being able to tell who's speaking because every character speaks exactly the same way the writer (or narrator of the story itself) speaks. And even if I do know who is speaking each time – because the writer tells me so – those characters have failed to come alive in my mind as I read, leaving me feeling as if I've somehow missed out on something good.

I had to do an assignment in Composition class once that really helped me with this. The assignment was to write two to three pages of dialogue with two people talking without using anything but dialogue. No "he said/she said," nothing explaining the sex or the emotions of the characters – I was to just let the dialogue do the talking. And the more my readers could tell about who was speaking, the higher my grade. It was really quite illuminating – and a lot of fun. So if you find that all of your characters speak with the same accent, using the same grammar and the same rhythm as you do, regardless of their age, sex, education, or the time in history they're living in, your manuscript has a good chance of being rejected – or at least edited to death. And your characters have certainly not come alive for you, or your reader, either.

WELL, WELL, WELL...

Another major pet peeve of mine is the use of "well" in a sentence. If I had my way, I would eliminate using "well" at all in anything but dialogue. And even there, I would use it sparingly.

I have had many writers defend their use of this word, especially in dialogue, saying that this is how people usually speak. And they may be right. Only using "well" over and over looks messy on the page and distracts from a good story. And when it's used in dialogue, it immediately takes me out of the story and reminds me that there is an author there speaking to me, instead of letting me forget that I'm being *told* a story. So just be aware, as you're writing, how often you use that word, and try to eliminate it as much as possible. Reading your work out loud is especially helpful in catching words that are overused.

HOW WE SPEAK

If you ever just listen to people speaking, you will notice that most of us do not always speak grammatically correctly; people will pause often, or repeat certain words (such as "oh," "um," "huh," etc.). And if you wish to make your dialogue realistic, there is a certain amount of that type of thing that is needed... even expected. But as I was taught in Scriptwriting class - by a professor who loved to embarrass me – that realistic dialogue often does not look very good on the page... and it is very distracting to read. (I was reminded of this when I rejected the script for *Rocky* because it sounded so incredibly stupid when I read it. Imagine reading Rocky Balboa's speech on the written page.) So yes, *do* try to be realistic when you are writing dialogue, while at the same time, remember that your audience is *reading* these words, and that too much of that realism can really turn your reader off. Example from Rocky:

I don't know. Would you like to maybe ...
you know, you and me... go out, you
know... together?

Of course, if you need to establish that a particular character is lower class, or has a speech impediment... or maybe he/she is five years old... then by all means, make your dialogue as realistic as possible. This goes along with not having the same voice for all of your characters – See KNOW YOUR CHARACTERS above.

RUN-ON SENTENCES

This is a habit that many of us fall into, unfortunately. It is very easy to make your sentences very long – with tons of commas, parentheses, or dashes – in order to get all the information that's in your head down on paper for your reader. But try to be selective as to what information you give away at one time… or rather, in the same sentence.

My personal rule of thumb is if you have to use more than one set of parentheses, more than three commas, or more than one "and" or "then," you may want to rethink your sentence structure. Keep in mind the REPEAT rule in Installment Three: always try to use variety in your sentence structure.

EXAMPLE of a run-on sentence:

It dropped sharply to within a couple of feet of the grass, and like a stunt pilot thrilling his audience, pulled out of the

nose dive at the last second, leveled off,
and headed for the street, barely missing a
large, white SUV with very dark windows
that was parked at the curb near our
mailbox.)

Technically, there is nothing wrong with this sentence. But it might sound better if it were written this way:

EXAMPLE:
It dropped sharply to within a couple of
feet of the grass. Like a stunt pilot thrilling
his audience, it pulled out of the nose dive
at the last second, leveled off, and headed
for the street, barely missing a large, white
SUV that was parked at the curb near our
mailbox.

I REPEAT... DON'T REPEAT

Too often, one of the biggest problems a manuscript will have is repeating. Whether it's starting sentences with the same word; the overuse of words such as "well," "um," "though," "whenever," "even," "therefore," or "wherefore"; using "said" after all dialogue; or using the same sentence structure. These are all pitfalls to avoid.

EXAMPLES of repeating:

a) *He looked into the sky. He stretched his arms. He looked toward the door.*

b) *"Well, I... um... I can't imagine, um...I... well... what can we do?*

c) *"How are you doing that? he said.*
   "I'm making it move with my mind," she said.
   "I want to give it a try," he said.

22

d) Walking to the door, he opened it and peered outside. Looking out, he didn't see anything. Peering closely, he noticed a light was out at the end of the hall.

Now, as is so often the case, there are exceptions to these rules. Sometimes you may choose to repeat something to make a point, or to build tension, or for humorous effect. If you are careful and don't abuse it, repeating can be a very effective tool.

More on I REPEAT, DON'T REPEAT
(Similar Sentence Structure)

It's so very easy to fall into a pattern when you write, one in which all of your sentences have the same structure.

EXAMPLE:
Drying her hair, she looked into the mirror and gazed at herself. Noticing a pimple, she promptly turned off the hair dryer to cover it with makeup. Noticing the sink was wet, she first cleaned that up before continuing to dry her hair.

As you can see, every sentence above starts with the same type of phrase. This quickly becomes irritating to your editor, and especially to your reader. To say the exact same thing, you can change the above to the following:

EXAMPLE:
As she dried her hair, she looked at herself in the mirror. Oh no, a pimple! Promptly, she turned off the hair dryer and went in search of her makeup case. Before she could start on that, she noticed the sink was wet, so she set about cleaning it. Was she ever going to get her hair dry?

To me, it's even more annoying when DIALOGUE is structured the same exact way, no matter who is speaking.

EXAMPLE:
"Can't we go to the store?" she asked. "I want to buy some hot dogs."
"Not right now," he said. "I'm tired."
"But that's not fair," she replied. "I'm hungry!"

Structuring your dialogue this way may seem straightforward and easy to read, but it's actually the opposite, as your reader will quickly start to see the flow and not even really pay attention to the storyline.

But more than that, this way of using dialogue doesn't tell us anything about your characters. And every bit of dialogue should both move you forward in the storyline, *and* tell you something more about who is speaking. This is what will keep your audience reading and wanting to know more. Here is how you can reconfigure this simple dialogue between two people to make it much more interesting… and much more fun to write as well.

EXAMPLE:
Carrie popped up between her mother and father in the front seat. "Can't we go to the store?" she asked as they neared the local market. "I want to buy some hot dogs."

Her father sighed. "Not right now, honey. I'm tired."

"But that's not fair. I'm hungry!" Carrie sat back and pouted.

Again with I REPEAT, DON'T REPEAT
(The under/overuse of Names)

This may seem like the same issue as "Too Much Name-Calling," but it's not. This one has to do with your characters referring to each other by name way too often when they speak to each other.

EXAMPLE:
"Honey, I'm home!"

Sarah ran up to her husband. "David, I missed you so much. How was your trip, honey?"

"It was long and tiring, darling. Can you get me a beer, sweetheart?"

"Of course, David."

If you spent some time in a public place, listening to people and how they speak in conversations with each other, you will see that they don't actually call each other by name too often. Perhaps in a situation where two people are *so* in love that they can't stop calling each other cutsie names, this might be useful (or comedic, as the case may be), but not in everyday dialogue. So unless your character is from another country, where people use more formal language – or another planet, where they obviously would speak differently from us – it's best not to have your characters refer to each other by name too often, even if that name is an endearment (honey, sweetheart, cutie, etc.) Be careful about this in your narrative, as well as in dialogue, as both can quickly become irritating to your reader.

EXAMPLE:
Zeke was a complicated man. Zeke was both quiet and explosive. No one quite knew how to handle Zeke from one moment to the next.

FIRST AND LAST NAMES

Another pet peeve for me is having someone introduce each new character using both their first and last names, and then continue to do this throughout the story. Again, there may be a particular purpose for this – your character may be foreign or an alien and that is how he or she speaks. But otherwise, there is no need to use both the first and last names over and over within a story. This does pertain to the "repeat" rule. But more than that, it says to your reader that you don't think they are smart enough to remember the last name of a person; and it's just plain annoying.

If you have a problem with two characters who have the same first name, as may happen occasionally in real life, you need to find a better way to distinguish between the two characters when explaining who are they are. You could use a Number 1 and Number 2 deal; a big John or little John thing; or give one or both of them a nickname, or shorten it, or even change the spelling (Debi and Debbie). And if none of those seems to work, change one of your characters' names (with the exception of nonfiction work, of course).

DON'T SAY IT – SHOW IT

Unless you are writing a script, where your actors need to know *how* something is said, a writer needs to *show* us how something is done instead of telling us outright. This applies in two areas:

    a) First, in dialogue, there is no need to tell us how a person is speaking if you've already made it obvious within the dialogue itself.

EXAMPLE:
"Mandy, oh my God, get away from him!" she said, scared for her.

Simply eliminate the "scared for her" part, since the dialogue has made that fact obvious to your reader.

    b) Use your characters' ACTIONS to tell us more about them, instead of just telling us.

31

EXAMPLE:
He was cautious and particular, needing everything in its place.

A better way to show us this would be something like:

EXAMPLE:
He stood before the mirror and combed his hair, adjusted his tie just so, then buttoned his jacket, the same as he did every morning. One more look at the clock before taking his coat off the coat rack and he was ready to go – right on schedule.

As always, there may be times when it's better to tell us instead of show us, but its best to keep this in mind as a general rule.

HE SAID/SHE SAID

One of the things that was pounded into me in my first writing class was that using "said" after dialogue is usually better than using anything else. Words such as "yelled," "whispered," "explained," "told," etc., can often be distracting and unnecessary. The only real exception to this rule would be in someone is asking a question or obviously yelling… then you could use "she asked" or "he yelled." Try not to get fancy and use words like "proclaimed" or "shouted" too often. This is part of the "Don't Repeat" rule, but it also follows the "Show – Don't Tell" rule; where you don't need to use those fancier words if you've told us enough in the dialogue itself.

EXAMPLE:
"Don't go over there, Rachel!" he screamed. "I need to check the locks first."

In this example, you should change "screamed" to said or eliminate the tag altogether.

You can also eliminate many of the "he said/she said" tags – they're called "dialogue tags" – in general, as long as you make sure that your readers know who is speaking. This is especially true when only two people are speaking; you need to tell us who is speaking only every now and then.

EXAMPLE:
Brad walked up to Cindy. "I love you, you know," he said.

Cindy put her arms around Brad. "I never doubted that for a second," she said.

There is no need for the "he said" or "she said" here, both because the rest of the sentence told us this, and because only two people are speaking.

MORE on HE SAID/SHE SAID

One of my biggest pet peeves is when someone repeatedly uses the same sentence structure... especially the whole "he said/she said" tag deal. If you are writing a lot of dialogue, I realize it is tempting to make sure your reader knows exactly who is speaking, as well as *how* he or she is speaking. And if you've read my previous installments, you may have systematically started replacing the instances of "she yelled" and "he proclaimed" and changing those to the simpler "he said/she said." And that's to be commended... to a point. Because constantly using the "he said/she said" tag after every single sentence, especially in the same place in a sentence, can be just as distracting... even annoying.

INCORRECT EXAMPLE:
"Hi," he said.
"Hiya," she said.
"What are you up to?" he said.
"Not much. How about you?" she said.

Here is how you can spice up just that small piece of dialogue:

CORRECT EXAMPLE:
"Hi," Brian said to Amy.
Amy smiled. "Hiya."
"What are you up to?"
"Not much." She gestured for him to sit.
"How about you?"

As you can see, the sentence structure has been varied just a bit – I was even able to add a bit of action to the scene, which is always preferable – and the "he said/she said" has been reduced enough so as to be barely noticeable within the dialogue itself.

NOTE: This cannot be stated enough: If you have only two people speaking, there is no need to use each person's name repeatedly.

36

RESTATING THE OBVIOUS

One pet peeve I've always had when I'm reading is redundancy, especially in dialogue. By this I mean telling us something more than once, which shows your reader that you are not confident enough that you've explained yourself well enough in your writing for him or her to get it the first time.

EXAMPLE:
"What kind was that?" Sam was curious.

The nature of the question tells us that Sam was curious. So wipe out that last sentence entirely. The exception would be if there was a *reason* for us to be told again that Sam was curious. For instance, maybe Sam isn't usually curious, so it's worth telling your reader how amazing it is that Sam was finally curious about something.

A few classic EXAMPLES:
"I agree," he added agreeably.

or:
"I'm sorry," she apologized.

For what should be obvious reasons, this is not really considered good writing.

As a general rule, let your dialogue do the talking (pun intended). Remember the repeat rules (in installment #3); but more than that, it's important that you don't assume that your reader can't understand the emotion within the dialogue. If you do it right, your dialogue can tell you everything you need to know about your characters' emotions.

EXAMPLES:
"Get out of my house!" (anger)
        or:
"Oh my god, what are you doing here?" (fear, surprise)

And remember, you can always use action outside of the dialogue to tell your reader even more instead of using a dialogue tag:

Using the EXAMPLES above:
"Get out of my house!" Greta slammed the door after him hard enough for the walls to shake. (anger)

"Oh my god, what are you doing here?" Sheila pulled the towel tighter around her body, trying to hide her trembling hands. She couldn't imagine how he found her. (fear, surprise)

I "SAID" ACTION!

A little more needs to be said regarding dialogue. This follows with "Stating the Obvious" in number #2 above. Basically, as a writer, you should always choose *showing* over telling.

Here's an EXAMPLE of grammatically correct dialogue that just tells:

"Mom, how much longer?" Sally asked.
"Not much longer, hon. Try resting for a bit," her mother replied.
"But mom, I don't want to go there!" Sally whined.
"Hush, Sally! Not another word," her mother said.

Technically, there is nothing wrong with this dialogue. But it only told us what was said; it didn't *show* us much. (It also over-used dialogue tags.)

Try it again here:

*"Mom, how much longer?" Sally
whispered from the back seat of the car,
hoping not to wake her father.*

*"Not much longer, hon?" Sally's mother
sniffed softly and turned her head so her
daughter couldn't see the tears that
threatened to fall once again. "Try resting
for a bit."*

*Sally gripped her teddy bear tightly. "But
mom, I don't want to go there!" She had
never seen a dead person before.*

*"Hush, Sally! Not another word." Sally
gulped when she saw her father's tears
start to fall again. Now she'd done it.*

ITALICS vs. UNDERLINING

One of my personal pet peeves is when someone uses underlining instead of italics. When I was in high school, I do remember that we used underlining a lot more often, but today it seems to be frowned upon more often than not.

Generally speaking, italics and underlining tend to *mean* the same thing. But it's still best to follow the most accepted rules of italics and underlining whenever possible, to avoid having your manuscript being rejected.

You use italics for the following:

Journals and Magazines: *USA Today*
Plays: *Madam Butterfly*
Long musical pieces: Tchaikovksy's *Nutcracker Suite*
Movie, television and radio titles: *Pirates of the Caribbean, Seinfeld, Car Talk*
Artworks: *Venus de Milo*

Famous speeches: Lincoln's *Gettysburg Address*

Long poems: Milton's *Paradise Lost*

The names of vehicles: *Titanic*
 (not to be confused with the brand, such as Ford)

Foreign words and phrases:

For emphasis: *"Coma esta usted?"* Mary asked.
 (unless they have become so common as to be part of our language, such as *et cetera*)

Of course, always be careful not to overuse italics for emphasis, as it will quickly lose its effect.

But no matter what, do not use *both* underlining and italics for the same word or phrase. It looks messy and it's very unprofessional.

DIALOGUE vs. NARRATIVE

I think my biggest pet peeve today is reading a book told from an omniscient author point of view, and then suddenly being pulled out of the story when the author decides to talk to me as if we're having a one-on-one conversation.

This seems to be a confusing issue for many writers today. When you are writing a story, in most cases, you are the omniscient author – meaning you know everything that's going on; everything about all of your characters; what is going to happen next, what your characters are thinking, as well as what went on before in your characters' lives. And this is how it should be. Your job, if you are doing it right, is to make your reader forget you are telling the story enough so that she can get into what is happening with your characters and make it her own. But that flow can so easily be thrown off when you, the storyteller, suddenly say." something like

"Guess what?" or "You guessed it...." or "I bet you didn't see that coming," etc. I call that turning your narrative into dialogue.

Now, if you are writing a story that is being told by one of your characters, that changes things. Then, of course, that character is going to be telling the story from his/her point of view, and often it is told as if that one character is talking directly to you, the reader, and no one else. It may be written in another dialect, or from someone a different age from you; perhaps even the opposite sex from you. And that's perfectly fine. That type of narrative is *also* dialogue of a sort.

One example that immediately comes to mind is from the book (and movie) *The Princess Bride.* In that story, the grandfather comes in and sits next to his grandson and opens a book: he's about to tell him a story. The story itself is then written from the point of view of an omniscient author, since he's reading the story from a book another author had written. But occasionally, the story will stop and switch back to the boy and his grandfather sitting in the room talking about the story. And that becomes more like dialogue, even though those two characters are still part of the story of *The Princess Bride*. It's a great example of how switching from narrative to dialogue can "pull you out" of the story (which in that case was intentional).

It's not grammatically incorrect to add things like "You know what?" and such in the story. Just be very aware of the type of story you're trying to tell and the mood you're trying to create. Because if you are writing as an omniscient author, your job is to step back and let the reader get sucked into the story, and to tell it from the point of view of the characters and let the *action* tell the story... not *you* as if you're talking to the reader directly. Unless that is your intention in the first place. Just be consistent either way. Because to me, there is nothing worse than being pulled out of a good story by having the author talk to me as if he/she's sitting next to me. It just ruins the mood.

"AND THEN"

This section is less about "then" versus "and" as it is about using either one at all. For the most part, "and" and "then" can be interchangeable, at least in terms of describing something that is happening in a particular order.

EXAMPLE:
This morning, I walked the dog, took a shower, and ate breakfast.

This sentence could also read:
"...*then* ate breakfast" without being incorrect grammatically.

But it seems that many writers like to use *both* "and" and "then" at the same time (or rather, one right after the other), and this is simply redundant and never needed (unless one of your characters speaks this way).

EXAMPLE:
I went to the store <u>and then</u> stopped for a bite to eat.

You can take out the "and" or the "then," since both are grammatically correct. But using both is just wordy and unnecessary.

ALL CAPS FOR EMPHASIS

Unless you are writing copy for a radio or television announcement, the use of all caps, even if it's for emphasis, is not only unnecessary, it is actually highly frowned upon. Today is the digital age, where everyone talks to each other via email and texts, so most people read all caps as yelling, and that is not pleasant to hear when you read.

If you need to emphasize something, you can italicize it. The only exception to this rule would be in dialogue, when someone is in an extreme or dangerous situation.

EXAMPLE:
"BRIAN, MOVE!!!" Carrie screamed.
The creature was right behind him.

Even so, if you are writing a story where there are a lot of intense situations like this, you shouldn't use all caps too often. Because even if it didn't completely turn off your reader, the other effect it could have is desensitizing your reader, causing your reader to almost ignore the meaning of the caps entirely.

DIALOGUE and NEW PARAGRAPHS

Something new I have started to notice in the manuscripts I'm editing is that many authors will choose to start a new paragraph when a character is speaking, no matter what the circumstance. And this is not always necessary.

EXAMPLE:
Mary turned toward the window and looked outside. "Did you see that?"

Since the same character is looking out the window, and she is speaking about what she sees outside the window, the dialogue can follow in the same paragraph.

EXAMPLE:
Mary turned toward the window and looked outside. "Did you see that?"

This not only reduces the need for dialogue tags (he said/she said), but this makes it easier for the reader to stay connected to what's happening in the story. Otherwise, your reader might think that someone else said, "Did you see that?" and get confused.

You can also add more action after the dialogue without creating a new paragraph … as long as that same character is the one doing the action:

EXAMPLE:
Mary turned toward the window and looked outside. "Did you see that?" She stood up to get a better look.

FLASH FORWARDS and
FLASHBACKS

There is no hard and fast rule regarding flash forwards and flashbacks for prose, other than that you use them sparingly. There is nothing more annoying – and confusing – then not being clear about where in time your characters are. I recommend starting a new chapter for each change in time, or at the least, making it very clear that something has changed, perhaps by using three spaces between paragraphs, changing into italics for a past or future event, or better yet, stating the year/time and/or place at the beginning of a section.

EXAMPLE:
Two days earlier
    or:
Mars, the year 3000

SOUNDS DON'T SPEAK

This is a pet peeve that creeps into a writer's work that is rarely discussed, so I thought it would be a good idea to mention it here. When you are using a sound within the context of your story, such as *BANG!* or *WHAM!,* the most acceptable way is to write them as I did here, capitalized and in italics. Do NOT use quotation marks, unless, of course, one of your characters is actually *saying* the word "bang" or "wham" to describe something.

Many people have also asked me if a sound word should have its own paragraph. I don't think that's necessary... unless you want that sound to be especially dramatic within the context of your story. Either way, try to be consistent if you use sound words often throughout your manuscript.

NUMBERS

A big pet peeve for me is a sentence that starts with a number – and the number is actually the number—that is, a numeral—instead of the spelling of the number. If you start a sentence with a number, *always* spell the number out. Or better yet, try to rearrange your sentence so that the number can be within the sentence instead.

> Incorrect: *"10-4, good buddy."*
> Correct: *"Ten-four, good buddy."*

Here are a few very basic things to remember about the use of numbers:

a) Spell out single digit numbers; use the actual number for those numbers greater than nine in magazines and greater than 100 in books.

EXAMPLES:
I want five copies.
  or:

I want 10 copies.

    b) Always spell out simple fractions, and use hyphens:

EXAMPLE:
One-half of the class took the test.

    c) *Be consistent within a category. If you choose numerals because one or more of the numbers is greater than nine, use numerals for all the numbers in that category.*

EXAMPLE:
Ten of the clocks were sold, but there are fifteen left.

If you choose to spell out the numbers because one of them is a single digit number, then spell out the rest of the numbers.

EXAMPLE:
On graduation day, four students earned fifteen honors each.

TO CAPITALIZE OR NOT TO CAPITALIZE

In most instances, if you've gone past the first grade, you know when to capitalize a word. But that's just talking about at the beginning of a sentence. What about the names of people, places and things? Here are a few hard and fast rules to follow regarding capitalization (besides the obvious ones):

a) Capitalize the first words in a quoted sentence.

EXAMPLE:
The principal stepped up to the podium and said, "Welcome, graduating class of 2012."

b) Capitalize a person's title when it follows the name on a person's address or signature line.

EXAMPLE:
Mr. Smith, Chairman.

    c) Capitalize the titles of high-ranking government officials when used before their names. Do not capitalize the civil title if it is used instead of the name.

EXAMPLE:
The president will address Congress. All senators are expected to attend.

    d) Capitalize any title when used as a direct address.

NOTE: This does NOT include the use of endearments such as "sweetheart," "honey," etc.

EXAMPLES:
"Will you take my temperature, Doctor?"
"I don't want to go to school, Dad."
"I'm going to bed, sweetheart."

e) Capitalize points of the compass only when they refer to specific regions.

EXAMPLE:
We are reading about the pioneers who went West. "Go west on Route 3 for three miles."

f) Do not capitalize seasons (unless the word is the start of a sentence.)

TO BE OR NOT TO BE...
Words that aren't really words

Occasionally I come across a word that is not actually a word. This usually happens because a writer is trying to be precise in how a word sounds when someone is speaking.

Incorrect EXAMPLE:
 "Uuuuuu... that's gross!"

Correct EXAMPLE:
"Ewww, that's gross!"

Even if the sound you picture in your head as you write is closer to the "Uuuuu" sound, it's always best to use the tried and true expression, as that is the one that the reader will recognize and interpret accordingly. Otherwise, you may confuse your reader and actually make her stop reading to look up this unexpected word or phrase she has never heard before. The only exception that would be acceptable is if your character cannot pronounce a certain word for an obvious reason. Perhaps he or she has a speech impediment, or she is three years old and hasn't learned the acceptable way to say a certain word or phrase... or English isn't his first language.

NOTE: Obviously, if you are writing a screenplay and you want to make sure your actor actually pronounces the word specifically like that, then that is what you would use. If not, stick with the normal spelling of the word.

WHAT'S IN A NAME?

Have you ever read a book where a few of the main characters' names are so similar that you confuse them, sometimes having to go back to see who the author is speaking about? This often happens when a writer gives two or more people the same name or names that are too similar to be easily distinguished. One of the most famous examples of this is from the book *The Lord of the Rings* by J.R.R. Tolkien, where he breaks this rule by calling Aragorn's love interests Arwen and Eowyn (they don't look exactly alike on the page, but they are pronounced nearly exactly the same). And he does it again by calling two of the bad guys Saruman and Sauron. Personally, this last one had me quite confused while I was reading the story; it was only after I had seen the movie trilogy that it made sense who was who.

Have you ever changed the name of a character in your head because you couldn't figure out how the name was supposed to be pronounced? One of the most famous of these, for me, was the main female protagonist in the Harry Potter books, Hermione Granger. I couldn't for the life of me figure out how to pronounce her name, so I changed it in my head to Heady while I was reading. Thankfully, once the movies came out, I got to hear how her name was supposed to be pronounced, but I would've much preferred that the author, at least once, let me know how that name was supposed to sound. (NOTE: If you do not want to include the pronunciation in the body of the word, you could do a list of characters with the pronunciation for each there. This is either at the beginning or very end of the book, and the characters can be listed alphabetically or in order of appearance.)

If you do have to have one or more characters with a similar name, it's a good idea to establish as quickly as possible the difference between the two – and not just in looks or personality traits. A better idea is to give them a descriptor, such as Little John and Big John, or maybe one is Johnny and the other Jon... or better yet, give one or both of them a more easily distinguishable nickname.

More on WHAT'S IN A NAME?
(too much name-calling)

Something else to look out for when you are referring to your character is giving them too many different names. Sure, it's fine for your characters to have nicknames. And there's certainly no problem with having one character call another something that means something just to him/her...

EXAMPLE:
"Hey there, sport fan, how's it going?" his father said.

But it does become a problem if the same person refers to another with many different pseudonyms, whether those are actual names (Angelica, Angel, Angie) or endearments (honey, sweetheart, sugar, love, etc.), even if that is the special name, as in the example above. If you purposely create a character who does this as one of his/her personality traits, and it's meant to mean something in the context of your story, that's one thing. But otherwise, the over-use of different names in referring to the same person can be distracting to downright annoying, so just be careful about that.

DEATH BY DIALOGUE TAG

This probably should've gone closer to the front of the book, since the improper use of dialogue tags is the biggest of my personal pet peeves as an editor.

As always, try to avoid redundancy, and keep it simple.

The biggest problem I find in most manuscripts is when the author tells us what the dialogue has already said:

EXAMPLE:
"I'm tired," he yawned.

It should go without saying that the tag here should be completely eliminated, as it's completely unnecessary.

Here are a few other common dialogue tag mistakes:

a) Use the SUBJECT before the verb when at all possible:

Incorrect EXAMPLE:
"I want to go home," said Sally.

Correct EXAMPLE:
"I want to go home," Sally said.

b) Do not use your dialogue tag to over-explain your character's actions.

Incorrect EXAMPLE:
*"Do you smell something?" **Betsy asked**, wrinkling her nose.*

Correct EXAMPLE:
"Do you smell something?" Betsy wrinkled her nose.

c) Do not use unnecessary dialogue tags.

A common mistake for new writers is to want to give credit to every single thing a character says. This is not necessary. The idea is to write the dialogue and other action so well that it's obvious who is speaking most of the time.

Incorrect EXAMPLE:
John grabbed the letter from Mary. "You don't want to read that," he said.

Correct EXAMPLE:
John grabbed the letter from Mary. "You don't want to read that."

d) Over-explaining the dialogue tag.

This rule goes with the "SHOW – DON'T TELL" rule that is drummed into every writer in their first writing class. Basically, if you have established the personality of your characters well, and you use your dialogue wisely, there should be no reason to give your reader additional information after the dialogue... unless, course, you are using it to specifically stress a point you want to get across that wasn't already made obvious.

Incorrect EXAMPLE:
"I... I... you are being so mean! I want to go home," Carolyn sobbed, her voice catching.

Correct EXAMPLE:
"I...I... you are being so mean. I want to go home," Carolyn sobbed.

e) Do not use multiple dialogue tags. To me, there is nothing more frustrating – and distracting – then telling me that a person is speaking... and then telling me AGAIN... especially when this is done throughout the entire manuscript.

Incorrect EXAMPLE:
"You cannot leave this house," he screamed as he went past her to the door and promptly locked it, saying, "I won't allow it."

Correct EXAMPLE:
"You cannot leave this house," he screamed. He went past her to the door and promptly locked it. "I won't allow it."

Incorrect EXAMPLE:
He said, "I want to invite you to a party." He gave her the invitation and added, "Will you come?"

Correct EXAMPLE:
He said, "I want to invite you to a party." He gave her the invitation. "Will you come?"

HEAD-HOPPING or POINT-OF-VIEW (POV)

One of the biggest sins new writers commit – and one of the pet peeves most complained about by editors and agents—is head-hopping, or changing the point of view within your story.

Many authors tend to write from the omniscient point of view, since this is the easiest way to tell us what all the characters are doing, more like the way you would view the story as if you were seeing it on a movie screen. As the omniscient author, you can even occasionally tell us what a character is thinking... while you are not part of the story yourself (in other words, you are not one of the characters in the story who is telling us what's happening). But if you choose to use the *first person* (as if you are the protagonist) or the *limited third* (where the story is written from the viewpoint of one or more of the characters in the story), do not suddenly change to

74

omniscient author, or vice versa. It's very distracting, and the quickest way to pull your reader out of the story as he/she wonders what is going on. Basically, if you choose to tell the story for one or more of the characters in your book, and you want to switch to omniscient author or to the viewpoint of another character, just make sure not to suddenly let us know what your characters are thinking. Use a visual cue to indicate the switch, such as an extra line space or a typographical device such as a line with three centered asterisks, and do not do it often or keep switching back and forth after only a few lines from one character's viewpoint to another's. This should help to avoid the problem of head-hopping.

EXAMPLES OF VIEWPOINT:

FIRST PERSON:
I gave a small shrug. That was of no matter at the moment.

THIRD PERSON:
Isaiah gave a small shrug. That was of no matter at the moment.

OMNISCIENT:
Isaiah gave a small shrug. He thought it was of no matter at the moment.

If this is still confusing for you, I highly recommend taking a writing class or purchasing a book on editing and grammar.

TO QUOTE OR NOT TO QUOTE

One of my newest pet peeves is the tendency for some writers to put various words into quotes to either stress their importance or otherwise show them off.

EXAMPLE:
My mother went to the "grocers" yesterday.

This type of quotation of a word or phrase is called an Apologetic Quotation Mark, and it's completely unnecessary. If you are stressing that a word is being used in a context where it shouldn't be, or it's a word that's not normally used (as in the example above) it's better to either put it into italics, or better yet, rephrase the sentence so that it's not needed.

EXAMPLE:
My mother's weekly visit to the grocer (she refused to call it a grocery store) went without a hitch.

THE END?

Many authors tend to use the words "The End" at the end of their manuscript.

Many editors prefer that a manuscript has "The End" at the end of their manuscript so that he or she will know that it is the end and that there are no missing pages, but it will generally be deleted before a book is published.

The general rule of thumb that I've seen is that historical fiction usually ends as such, but more modern fiction does not. So don't be offended if your edited manuscript comes back with "The End" missing.

GRAMMAR

"A scrupulous writer, in every sentence that he writes, will ask himself at least four questions, thus:
1. What am I trying to say?
2. What words will express it?
3. What image or idiom will make it clearer?
4. Is this image fresh enough to have an effect?"

~ George Orwell, "Politics and the English Language"

STYLE vs. FORM
WHEN IS GRAMMAR IMPORTANT?

I have often been made fun of by my children if they catch me speaking grammatically incorrectly (although I am proud of the fact that they actually notice). They've also asked me why I don't always correct them when they do the same (although admittedly, I do joke about their incorrect grammar at times). And I have always told them that it's not as important to me that someone *speak* grammatically correctly – unless they are in a situation that warrants it (such as speaking to a prospective employer), because people don't speak grammatically correctly... for the most part.

That said, I tend to agree completely with Margaret Shertzer's quote in her book, *The Elements of Grammar,* when she says, "While informal speech commonly uses colloquial expressions, few people wish to appear illiterate in their speaking or writing." Basically, what this means is, unless the *narrator* of your story is an illiterate, for whatever reason (the time period or place he or she is born in, for instance), you as the writer have a duty to write your story using correct grammar, even if the characters in your story don't speak that way. So even if your dialogue is full of incorrect grammar, you should make sure that the rest of the story is written with correct grammar.

THAT vs. WHICH

Per request, I'm going to cover the dilemma most of us have of choosing between "that" and "which." It seems that these two words have begun to be interchangeable, when they most definitely are not supposed to be.

Basically, the word "that" is used in a restrictive clause and the word "which" is used in a non-restrictive clause.

To put it in layman's terms, use "that" to *define* a specific thing being referred to.

For instance, you can say either: *the house that was hideous or that hideous house.*

When you use "which," anything that follows is extra and not essential to the meaning of the sentence.

EXAMPLE:
She entered that hideous house, which was not what he expected her to do.

Please note that you *always* use a comma before "which" but not before "that," since anything that follows after "that" is essential to the sentence.

An editor friend of mine has a mnemonic (memory device) she uses to help her in always using the right one: If a sentence tells you *which* one it was, you *don't* want "which"; you want "that." If it *doesn't* tell you *which* one it was, you *do* want "which." It's the exact reverse of what you'd expect.

PASSIVE VOICE vs. ACTIVE VOICE

This is one of the trickiest parts of writing, and some editors get really upset when they see the passive voice being used rather than the active. So you really need to know the difference and when it is acceptable to use passive over active voice.

Simply stated, in a sentence using active voice, the subject of the sentence performs the action expressed in the verb.

EXAMPLE:
The cat bit the mouse.
 (the subject is "cat" and the action is "bit")

I have had many authors tell me that they choose passive voice – or don't worry about the use of passive voice – over active because that is how most of us speak (dialogue). And that is, unfortunately, very true. So like all fiction writing, your characters may speak quite differently from how you, the writer, would speak when telling the story. This is how you can tell the difference between the writer and the characters in a story. So it's good to be aware of the difference between active and passive voice and to know when is the best time to use each. And before submitting to a publisher or an editor, find out what his or her preference is in terms of active vs. passive voice.

Here is an example of passive vs. active voice:

PASSIVE: The book is being read by most of the class.
ACTIVE: Most of the class is reading the book.

One thing that sticks out in passive voice is the use of "by the" or "is being" types of phrases, which can make a sentence a bit more sloppy or harder to read.

MIXING TENSES

Probably one of the easiest problems to fall into as a writer is mixing tenses. And submitting a manuscript with this flaw is one of the prime causes for an editor to reject it. Make sure you always know if you are referring to your characters doing something in the *present* moment (present tense) – like right now – or if you are referring to something that happened previously (past tense) or will/might happen in the future (future tense) … and be consistent! This is especially crucial if you use flashbacks and flash-forwards in your manuscript.

The easiest tense to use is the *present tense*. The present tense is used when:

   a) The action is general:

EXAMPLE:
I live in New York.

b) The action happens all the time/habitually:

EXAMPLE:
John drives a taxi.

c) The action is not only happening now – it has happened, is happening, and will happen in the future:

EXAMPLE:
We meet every Thursday.

d) The statement is always true:

EXAMPLE:
The moon goes around the Earth.

This is not to be confused with the *past tense*. The past tense is used to talk about actions that happened at a specific time in the past. You make most verbs (action words) past tense by adding *–ed*. Of course there are exceptions, so-called "irregular verbs," which form their tenses differently, such as ride/rode and buy/bought.

EXAMPLE:
I worked on that project myself.

It gets more complicated when you use verbs that you can't add *–ed* to, but you get the picture:

EXAMPLES:
I <u>got</u> married last year.
            or:
When I was young, we <u>went</u> to England in the summer.

TOWARD vs. TOWARDS

My own personal pet peeve is using the word "towards" instead of toward. To me, "towards" sounds less sophisticated. I will occasionally use the word "towards" if it sounds better in the context of the story. But in actuality, there is no right or wrong – it's mostly personal preference.

The general rule is that if you are an American author and your characters are speaking English, "toward" without the additional 's' is preferred, while those in Britain most often use "towards."

CONJUNCTION JUNCTION, WHAT'S YOUR FUNCTION?

Many of you might remember the song "Conjunction Junction" from Schoolhouse Rock by Jack Sheldon. He said very simply in that catchy tune that the function of a conjunction (better known by all of us as *and*, *but*, and *or*, among others) is "hooking up words and phrases and clauses."

Conjunctions are also well known for eliminating the use of commas.

EXAMPLES:
I want to go home but my work isn't done yet. I bought her flowers and a vase for them to go in.

One of my pet peeves is using a conjunction *and* a comma, such as:

EXAMPLE:
I had peas, and corn, and green beans for lunch.

The only time it's correct to use a conjunction, such as *and*, with a comma is at the end of a list. Let's use the same example from the sentence above:

EXAMPLES:
I had peas, corn, green beans, and squash for lunch.
       or:
I had peas and corn and green beans for lunch.

One of the most frequently asked questions of editors – and one that is a pet peeve for many of them – is when to use a conjunction at the *beginning* of a sentence, such as "But they went without cereal" or "And they left her stranded." While the use of a conjunction at the beginning of a sentence is not exactly wrong grammatically, it should be used sparingly.

Before starting a sentence with an "and" or "but," it's best to ask yourself these questions:

a) Would the sentence/paragraph function just as well without the conjunction *and*

b) Should the sentence in question be connected to the previous sentence?

Of course, you need to consider if adding the sentence to the previous one would make the previous sentence a run-on sentence, or otherwise ruin the flow of the story. This may also be the way your character speaks or your narrator tells the story. As always, there are exceptions to every rule. But I would be careful to make sure your editor doesn't have a pet peeve about the use of conjunctions at the beginning of sentences if you are a fan of their use.

PUNCTUATION

*"Here is a lesson in creative writing. First rule: Do not use semicolons.
They are transvestite hermaphrodites representing absolutely nothing.
All they do is show you've been to college."*

~ Kurt Vonnegut, "A Man Without a Country"

COMMAS, COMMAS, COMMAS

Where to place or not place a comma can be very tricky. And truthfully, sometimes that can be a personal preference. But regardless of whether you are an over-comma user or rarely use commas at all, there are a few hard-and-fast rules you should keep in mind:

a) Always use a comma before someone else's name when you are using it to address them.

EXAMPLE:
"How are you today, Diana?" or *"I'm coming home, Dad."*

b) If you qualify a person who is speaking after dialogue (that is, if you follow a quotation with a dialogue tag), and you are not using an exclamation point or a question mark, you must use a comma... NOT a period.

EXAMPLE:

"I don't want to answer that question," she replied.

Always put a comma before "which" in a sentence.

EXAMPLE:

She ran to the door and threw it open, which is not what her husband expected.

MORE ON COMMAS

I think a major pet peeve for most editors is the over-use of commas. There are some writers who seem to just throw those pesky things everywhere, even in places where you would not normally pause. But on the other hand, there are those who rarely use them, even when they are needed, such as after dialogue. Both problems are just as annoying for an editor.

I tell all my authors that it is a great idea to read your work out loud – whether you have an audience or not – and pay attention to pausing wherever you have put a comma, and not pausing where you don't have one. This will really help you to get a feel for the flow of the words, whether it is dialogue or not. And if you find that you are putting more than two commas in any sentence, it may be a good idea to restructure it so that it flows better, even if that means creating a new sentence entirely.

EXAMPLE of over-use:
He was dressed, like always, unless he were nude, in one of his many expensive suits.

EXAMPLE of better use:
Unless he was nude, he was always dressed in one of his many expensive suits, as he was now.

As you can see in the examples above, you don't even have to change the content of the sentence to eliminate the over-use of commas.

A LITTLE MORE ON COMMAS

Lately, my biggest pet peeve has been the overuse, under-use or inconsistent use of commas when going through a manuscript. There are some instances when a comma does not have to be used:

EXAMPLE:
In the morning(,) we went swimming.

But more than that, if you use a comma after a prepositional phrase in one sentence, it is best to use it in the next. Consistency makes it easier for your editor to find and fix a mistake, as well as for your reader to get the feel for how you write.

I find that many writers don't seem to be sure as to whether or not they should use a comma after "and." And that can be tricky sometimes.

EXAMPLE:
I thought we should go to the park, check out the animals at the zoo, and maybe go to McDonald's for lunch afterwards.

In the example above, the comma before the "and" isn't really necessary, but if you tend to use the comma before an "and" in a list, use it every time.

~~~~~~~~

I've also noticed that many writers tend to forget to use a comma after dialogue.

EXAMPLE:
"I need to get going" Sally said.

That is simply bad writing. Some type of punctuation is always needed after dialogue.

~~~~~~~~

And another misuse of commas is when you use the three dots (called an ellipsis) and then a comma.

BAD EXAMPLE:
"I'm going to see if I can....,"

In this example, the dots *are* the punctuation at the end of the dialogue. The comma is not needed.

~~~~~~~~~~

Even more annoying is when someone seems to haphazardly place commas where there is no need for them, while also forgetting to use them where they should be.

EXAMPLE:
She came into my office, that day and saw what I was doing. She couldn't mistake the look, in my eyes, of a crazy person. My eyes were bloodshot my hair askew and my clothes disheveled.

As always, if you read a sentence out loud and pause only where the commas tell you to pause, you might more easily see where the breaks should be and where the commas are that need to be eliminated.

SEMICOLONS

Personally, I am a fan of the semicolon, especially if it reduces the use of "and" or "then" or the infamous dots called an ellipsis [...]. But as with any editing tool, they can be overused. So, as always, try to vary your sentence structure throughout your writing so that no particular type of sentence is overused (and therefore, predictable and boring).

The semicolon is used more in informal writing, such as in novel manuscripts or in dialogue. (The colon is used more for lists and such – more on the colon later.)

As a general rule, think of the semicolon as a replacement for "and" or "then," even though you can still use either of them after a semicolon. Often, what comes after a semicolon is a complete sentence of its own, but not always. I think of it this way: the semicolon is a way to put a slightly longer pause in a sentence without starting a new one. It keeps the flow of the sentence moving without the full stop of a period.

EXAMPLES:
A tiny spurt of joy lanced through her; she couldn't help but smile.
       or:
It was spiky, not soft; coarse, not fine.

Another use of the semicolon is to separate items in a list that contains commas within the items in the list.

EXAMPLE:
She wore her hat, which was red; her blouse, which was purple and very bright; a multi-colored bandana in her hair, the predominant colors of which were green and gold; and of course that peacock-and-lilac skirt, which had other colors in it as well.

DASHES

Oh, this pet peeve is a big one for me. Dashes are tricky. I personally tend to overuse them myself, so I'm very careful about them.

For this one, I feel I should reiterate the basic rules on when to use a dash – taken from *The Elements of Grammar* by Margaret Shertzer:

    a) Use a dash to indicate an abrupt change in a sentence

EXAMPLE:
"He said you would be, but—Omigod!" *

    b) Sometimes a dash is used to set off interpolated and explanatory matter

EXAMPLE:
She admired their acquisitions – the artwork, the wine, the occasional tan. *

c) Use a dash to indicate a sudden break in a sentence.

EXAMPLE:
After promising she'd stay in touch – a promise she had every intention of ignoring – Scout hung up the phone and threw it back into her bag.*

d) A dash may be used to set off a long phrase in apposition, particularly when a phrase is punctuated with commas.

EXAMPLE:
Something about his smile did seem vaguely familiar, but his eyes – the color of glass – cool, opaque, unfathomable – were those of a stranger.)*

e) A pair of dashes may be used instead of parentheses.

EXAMPLE:
Why, for the last few years, she'd felt like one of those migrating birds – the ones with the little magnetic particles in their heads – when winter would rear its head in her state.

As always, try not to over-use dashes, as they can become quite distracting, especially when nearly every sentence in your dialogue ends with a dash because a character never gets to finish speaking or another character may pause a lot in their speech and use dashes constantly. Variety is the key to more interesting writing (and reading).

NOTE: I do realize that often in real life, people repeatedly break into one another's' sentences when they talk, but when you read that on paper, with all those dashes or ellipses (triple dots), it becomes distracting. So try to eliminate that as much as you can in your writing.

The writing examples are from Scent of the Roses by P.G. Forte

DASHES vs DOTs (ellipsis)

There has been a running debate between those who use dashes and those who prefer three dots (ellipsis). Basically, neither one is better than the other, although more professional documents tend to use the dash, while the ellipsis should be used more often in less formal writing, such as dialogue.

In most cases, the ellipsis is used more to create a specific effect... in other words, they are put there as a pause to add just a tad bit of additional drama.

EXAMPLE:
I don't want to achieve immortality through my work...I want to achieve it through not dying. (Woody Allen)

COOL HINT: Confused about colons, semicolons and three dots? Use a dash. The dash performs all the functions of the colon, the semicolon and three dots.

Either way, be consistent throughout your manuscript. If you do occasionally mix them up in the same manuscript, NEVER use them together in the same sentence. There is nothing more distracting than seeing a bunch of dashes and dots throughout a manuscript while you are reading.

DASHES, PARANTHESES, COMMAS,
oh my!

I can't count how many times I've come to a sentence that incorporates dashes, along with parenthesis, and a ton of commas to boot. To me, if I look at a sentence – or even a group of sentences – quickly, and see that it has all of these within it, it looks haphazard and messy and I avoid reading it. If possible, try using more than one sentence to incorporate everything you have to say. Or at the very least, rearrange how the sentence is written so that it doesn't look so haphazard on the page. And try to restrict using all three of the above.

Here's an EXAMPLE of a haphazard sentence:
The monk (if pushed) can make that deadline. "DAMN IT!" He slammed his fist down on his desk, "I have spent the better part of my life.... I don't know what I'm going to do... Doctor!"

This is how you can easily fix this:

The monk believed he could make that deadline, if he was pushed. Damn it! He slammed his fist on his desk. "I have spent the better half of my life devoted to that man," he said to himself. "Doctor!"

Try reading your work out loud exactly how it's written. Don't interpret it the way you want it to sound or you won't see that on the page what you've written looks awkward and is therefore hard for your reader to read as well.

I DECLARE!
(When does one use EXCLAMATION
POINTS?)

I have been asked to give my opinion on the use of exclamation points. As you know, exclamation points are used to show that someone is yelling or overly excited. But they can definitely be overused. My basic rule of thumb regarding the use of exclamation points is to use them sparingly. Obviously, if someone is telling another person to "Look out!" when someone is going to attack them, etc., that is a good time to use one. But if someone is angry, you don't necessarily have to use an exclamation point after every sentence he/she speaks. And you definitely do *not* need to use more than one exclamation point.

You can also use the qualifiers after the sentence to say how upset someone is as an alternate to using an exclamation point

EXAMPLE of over-use:
"Joe! Joe! Get out of the way! I have to get to the door! Move it!"

Try this instead:

EXAMPLE:
"Joe, get out of the way," Brian panted. "I have to get to the door. Move it!"

NOTE: With emails, text messages and instant messages so prevalent today, the exclamation point is more and more often overly used; and those who communicate online so often (like me) actually "hear" someone yelling whenever exclamation points (or all caps) are used. Just something you should think about when you decide to use that exclamation point.

AND I QUOTE...

When someone is speaking, always use double quotation marks. I'm not sure why some people have started using single quotation marks for dialogue, but the only place that is acceptable is when someone is speaking and actually quoting what someone else has said – dialogue within dialogue.

EXAMPLE:
"Mom, listen to what my teacher writes: 'Max has been doing superb this year in Math class.'"

NOTE: The use of single quotations for dialogue does seem to be a standard in Britain and other European countries. But if you are American and your characters are using standard American English, stick with the double quotation marks.

More on AND I QUOTE
(the right use of quotation marks)

Lately, it seems as if many writers are starting to use single quotation marks (") instead of double quotation marks (" ") for dialogue to enclose a direct quotation. Unless you come from Britain, where single quotation marks for dialogue is the standard, you use single quotation marks only when you are using a quote within a quote.

EXAMPLE:
"And the man said to me, 'Give me all your money!'"

Here are some hard and fast rules regarding quotation marks:

a) Periods and commas always go *inside* quotation marks, even inside single quotes.

EXAMPLE:
"Hurry up," she said.

   b) If a question is in quotation marks, the question mark should be placed *inside* the quotation marks.

EXAMPLE:
She asked, "Will you still be my friend?"

   c) Use double quotation marks to enclose the titles of songs, short stories, essays, poems, and articles:

EXAMPLE:
She started to sing the words to "Bad Medicine" by Bon Jovi.

NOTE: Do *not* put quotation marks around the titles of books, newspapers, or magazines; instead, italicize or underline those titles.

ONE MORE THING…
or TWO

"One day I will find the right words, and they will be simple."

~ Jack Kerouac, "The Dharma Bums"

KEEP A WRITING JOURNAL

This is not a pet peeve, but I thought it was important to mention it anyway.

When I was in college, one of my professors asked the class to start a writing journal. This journal wasn't where we would write our stories, or even our ideas for stories. It was a journal we would keep with us whenever we read someone else's work. There, we would write down phrases, descriptions, meaningful dialogue... basically anything that struck us as brilliant, interesting or otherwise unique in some way. Try it! You'll be amazed at the gems you'll find. I still have mine and I enjoy looking it over now and then. And one day I hope to be in someone else's writing journal.

TO READ OR NOT TO READ

*"If you don't have time to read, you don't have the time
(or the tools) to write. Simple as that."*
~ Stephen King

The most surprising thing I have ever heard a writer tell me is that he/she doesn't read. *How can a writer not read?* I would ask. And I would be told that the person doesn't read because he or she is afraid of having her writing become too much like another writer's work...which is just ridiculous. I'm sorry, but it is incredibly obvious when you read a manuscript that is written by someone who doesn't read, especially in his or her particular field of writing. You can't read nonfiction work if you write only fiction, and vice-versa. Actually, you should read *all* kinds of work in order to become the best writer you can be. And unless you plan to become a plagiarist, stealing directly from someone else's work, you have nothing to worry about when it comes to becoming too much like a certain writer. For one, that might actually be a *good* thing: since quite often someone will pick up a book that has a similar style to another favorite author. So if you want to become a great writer, *read…* as often as you can, and in as many different styles and genres as you can. You will not only learn what type of styles you like – or dislike – but you will soak up the best ways to write without even realizing it. In my own writing composition class, I was once asked how I got straight A's in all my writing courses, while I had nearly failed my grammar test. It was because at the time I knew *how* to write the right way, while not necessarily knowing *why* that was the right way… because I had been an avid reader my entire life. (Of course, now I know both the how *and* the why.)

A NOTE FROM THE EDITOR

I hope you have enjoyed this book and found it very useful. I believe you can get something new from it every time you go through it. Of course, I also don't doubt that there are many other "peeves" out there that other editors have – and I welcome their comments – but these were the ones that I have found most often in my own work as an editor.

I cannot stress enough that there are exceptions to every rule. Write from the heart... write about what you know... do your research... don't worry so much about the right grammar and structure the first time around. Then, once you are done, read your work *out loud*, to yourself, or to an audience. That is the time to fix your grammar, eliminate or add punctuation, and work on tightening your work until it flows smoothly. And if that is not something that you believe you can do for yourself, by all means, *hire an editor*. A good editor won't detract from your work but will work *with* you to make your work shine. A good editor can help you to see holes in your story that you might have missed. But most of all, a good editor will not change your story into something he/she would prefer but instead will let you keep your own voice. And if you can find such an editor, treat him/her well, because that is a rare find, indeed.

Oh, and one more thing....

Never stop writing!

Debi Staples

SynergEbooks

Taking Books to New Heights

125

Made in the USA
Columbia, SC
04 March 2025

54701563R00074